Reflections of God

Meg Lacaria McCoy

Reflections of God

Copyright 2019 Meg Lacaria McCoy. All rights reserved.

No part of this book may be reproduced, stored in a retrieval system, or transmitted by any means without the written permission of the author.

Scripture quotations are taken from the *YouVersion Holy Bible.* Copyright 2008-2018 Life.Church, Developer:

New International Version, NIV

New King James Version, NKJV

Holman Christian Standard Bible HCSB

God's Word Translation GWT

The Message, MSG.

In honor of my Lord and Savior Jesus Christ.

This book Is dedicated to:

You

Maybe you are at the very beginning of an exciting journey into adulthood. Maybe you are starting out your new life in Christ. Maybe you just need to take a breath. Wherever you are in your journey, my prayer for you is that you always remember how much your Heavenly Father loves you and has a perfect plan for your life. He took great care to design you exactly the way you are — a cherished daughter who is beautiful inside and out. Never be afraid to go to Him for anything.

He is always as close as your heartfelt prayer.

The LORD himself goes before you and will be with you;
He will never leave you nor forsake you.
Do not be afraid; do not be discouraged.

Deuteronomy 31:8 NIV

Table of Contents

Chapter One — 1
In the beginning...

Chapter Two — 17
In His Image

Chapter Three — 29
Immanuel God with Us

Chapter Four — 49
Ishi, My Beloved

Chapter Five — 61
The LORD My Keeper

Chapter Six — 77
The LORD My Comfort

Chapter Seven — 95
The Alpha and Omega

*In the beginning
God created
the heavens
and the earth.*

Genesis 1:1 **NIV**

Look up.

God's presence is all around you.

Listen.

He whispers His love to you.

Marvel.

He paints the sky with colors He chose just for you.

Consider.

You see the beauty of nature in a slightly different way than others see it, because God knows *your* heart. He shows His love for you in ways that only you understand. Look into the face of a flower — so intricate, so fragile, so perfect. Created by your Father to bring you joy and delight.

When Adam and Eve were forced to leave Eden, God could have allowed His creation to decay into something horrible, reflecting its fallen state. But He didn't. He kept the beauty of nature so you would not lose heart.

And God said,
"Let there be light," and there was light.

Genesis 1:3 NIV

There is an innate understanding and acceptance of our Heavenly Father's existence in the heart of a child. God's Word reminds us that we should have this same heart, a heart that's open, trusting, loving.

DAWN
(as seen through the eyes of a child)

I got up early yesterday
to watch the darkness fade away.
The first faint rays were breaking through
to make a day all fresh and new.

I watched the flaming fireball rise,
lighting the world before my eyes.
Tranquil warmth enfolded me
and I was content to watch and see.

The birds in the treetops chirped away
and as I listened they seemed to say,
"To think that one God caused to be born
the magical wonders of early morn."

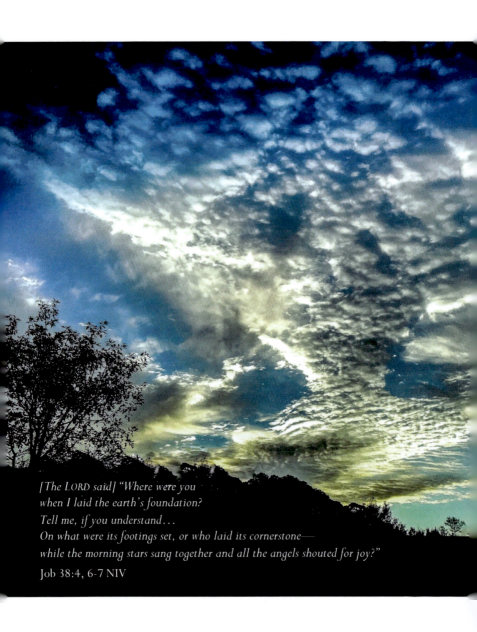

[The LORD said] "Where were you
when I laid the earth's foundation?
Tell me, if you understand...
On what were its footings set, or who laid its cornerstone—
while the morning stars sang together and all the angels shouted for joy?"

Job 38:4, 6-7 NIV

Close your eyes and imagine that you are present at the beginning. You are watching the Father, Son, and Holy Spirit orchestrate a most elaborate composition of perfection as, little by little, an incredibly beautiful scene emerges against a backdrop of star and angel accolades that echo throughout eternity.

Watch and listen as all creation worships the Creator. Trees lift branches in praise; flowers open their hearts to Him in complete surrender; and birds chirp melodious harmonies in concerts of adoration, all to accompany you as you offer yourself in worship to your Lord.

Proof of His love is all around you. Stop the busyness of your day. Close your eyes and give yourself to Him in adoration. Let Him refresh you and take your burdens. Breathe in His strength, His joy, His comfort. Breathe out the excess of His love to share with others.

This is the person He created you to be.

God is The *Breath* of Life. He spoke the world into being.

> *By the word of the LORD the heavens were made,*
> *their starry host by the breath of his mouth.*
>
> Psalm 33:6 NIV

Jesus is The *Word* of God. He was with God at creation.

> *He was with God in the beginning.*
> *The Word became flesh and made his dwelling among us.*
> *We have seen his glory, the glory of the one and only Son,*
> *who came from the Father, full of grace and truth.*
>
> John 1:2,14 NIV

The Comforter, the *Holy Spirit*, lives in the hearts of those who have given their lives to the Lord.

> *"And with that he [Jesus] breathed on them and said,*
> *"Receive the Holy Spirit."*
>
> John 20:22 NIV

From before the foundation of the world
all three existed as One:

God the **Father**   God the **Son**   God the **Holy Spirit**

A beautiful, glorious mystery, unseen but felt, like a breath of wind that brushes your cheek. As you draw in the Word of God, His Spirit will illuminate your soul with understanding.

She sat on the front porch, drinking in the breathtaking sight of God's vaulted night sky. Words that were impressed on her open heart tumbled down her arm into her hand and spilled out the tip of her pen onto the paper in her lap. After recording the words, she laid down the pen and marveled at the love of her Heavenly Father, which He poured out freely by His Holy Spirit, to bless the heart of one of His children…her.

O glorious light
that thrusts your beams of silver earthward!
What great Hand guides you
as you make your way across a velvet sky,
majestic in your silent journey
toward night's end.

What silent Whisper appoints your course
and counsels you to rim the clouds
with cold white fire.

The same Love that holds me
keeps you steadfast in the darkness
and clears the skies for you to
burst forth from your chains
and pour across the expanse of heaven,
drenching her with splendor
as you claim the night your own!

As you bid the hush of night "sweet dreams,"
remember the Love that displays itself in the skies above you
is the same Love that guides you throughout each day.

Your Father made all of it for you, His beloved child.
Even if you had been the only person on earth,
He still would have created all this beauty for you to enjoy.

All nature points to your Father, your Creator, the One who shows you how special you are in the intricacy of a snowflake, each one different but all beautiful, just like you!

Take the time to walk outside and breathe in the beauty of creation. Follow the sun as it rises in the morning or watch the moon climb a ladder of stars through the heavens at night; let your eyes feast on fall's riotous colors reflected in the stillness of a lake; or close your eyes and listen to the bees buzzing their way through a smorgasbord of nectar as birds serenade in the background.

The Father's love is deliberate and evident in the beauty of His created world, and it is freely lavished on all mankind. It is extravagant and without hesitation or reservation. He is a gracious God.

He waits patiently for you to love Him.

For since the creation of the world God's invisible qualities —
his eternal power and divine nature—have been clearly seen,
being understood from what has been made,
so that people are without excuse.

Romans 1:20 NIV

My Favorite Places to Experience God

So God created mankind

in his own image,

in the image of God

he created them;

male and female

he created them.

Genesis 1:27 **NIV**

Then God said,
"Let us make mankind in our image, in our likeness."

Genesis 1:26a NIV

Adam was created out of the dust of the ground. God breathed His life into Adam and thus became part of Adam.

Just think — God *breathed* into Adam and gave him life. The first human being from whom all mankind came. Does that mean that all people since Adam have God's breath in them? Is this why we sometimes feel empty and incomplete? Could our loneliness be caused by the yearning in our hearts to be reconciled with our Heavenly Father, our Creator, the One who breathed life into us?

Only God can help us find and become our true selves, the unique people He created us to be. His Word spills the truth of changed lives throughout history, the pages illuminated by the footprints of Spirit-filled people who found their true selves in Him.

We can KNOW God, not just know about Him. From the time we first accept God's free gift of salvation, paid for by the blood of His Son, our Heavenly Father carefully begins the polishing process. Throughout our lives, He continues to polish and buff away those things that enslave us, until we are polished to a brilliant reflection of Himself.

*"For you created my inmost being;
you knit me together in my mother's womb.*

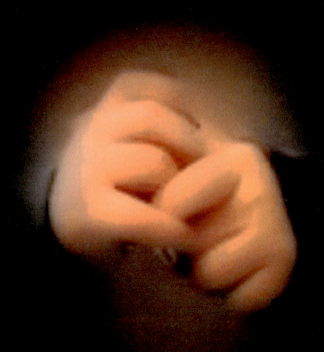

*I praise you because I am fearfully and wonderfully made;
your works are wonderful, I know that full well."*

Psalm 139:13-14 NIV

Tiny hands, helpless but perfect in the eyes of the One
Who created them.

The word of the LORD came to me, saying,
"Before I formed you in the womb I knew you,
before you were born I set you apart;"

Jeremiah 1:4-5a NIV

Hands designed for specific work to point others to a loving Father.

For we are God's handiwork,
created in Christ Jesus to do good works,
which God prepared in advance for us to do.

Ephesians 2:10 NIV

Watch a child — innocent, trusting, loving.

He called a little child to him,
and placed the child among them.
And he said: *"Truly I tell you,*
unless you change and become like little children,
you will never enter the kingdom of heaven.
Therefore, whoever takes the lowly position of this child
is the greatest in the kingdom of heaven.
And whoever welcomes one such child in my name
welcomes me."

Matthew 18:2-5 NIV

EVERY LIFE, WITHOUT EXCEPTION, IS PRECIOUS IN HIS SIGHT.

For you created my inmost being;
You knit me together in my mother's womb.

Psalm 139:13 NIV

Safe in the Master Potter's Hands

Rough and unformed, but in the skilled hands of your Heavenly Father, a glorious work of art will eventually emerge. A lengthy process, a difficult process, and at times you might feel as though parts of you are literally being torn off, the pain of becoming like your Lord almost more than you can bear.

You might wonder if it's worth it, if this constant stripping away of the person you think you are is really necessary. Do you really have to "pass through the fire"?

As the clay has to be fired to make it strong enough to hold its form, the Potter refines those He loves with the fire of testing, of trials, of hardship. He knows how each will come out on the other side, knows exactly what is needed because He went through the fire first. His love will guide and protect you in the midst of trials so that you, as His precious child, will grow into the work of art He designed you to be.

"For I know the plans I have for you," declares the LORD,
"plans to prosper you and not to harm you,
plans to give you hope and a future."

Jeremiah 29:11 NIV

God has a perfect plan for your life, a plan that will bring you joy and fulfillment and Him honor and glory. He sent His Son to walk beside you. When you put Him first in your life, you will seek Him when you come to a fork in the road and you have to make a choice. As His child, you always have access to Him, and His Holy Spirit will guide you.

As you seek the Lord's will for your life, the time you spend every day with Him alone, *just the two of you*, will cause your spirit to expand and soar. He is your Best Friend. As you trust Him more and more with the details of your life, things that challenge you will be easier to face, knowing the Holy Spirit is guiding you. With His hand on your life, you will never be alone. Like He was with David, your Lord will be there to fight your battles for you. Like Peter, when you keep your heart focused on Jesus, He will be next to you, holding you up in the midst of the stormy sea.

God loves all of us. It's humbling to think that He loves those who hate Him just as much as He loves you and me. It's also an opportunity to share in His sufferings by following His example and loving others who may not love you in return. This brings honor to Him and opens the door for you to point someone to a saving relationship with Christ.

> *Jesus replied:*
> *"Love the Lord your God with all your heart*
> *and with all your soul and with all your mind.*
> *This is the first and greatest commandment.*
> *And the second is like it:*
> *Love your neighbor as yourself."*

Matthew 22:37-39 NIV

How I See Me

_____
_____
_____
_____
_____
_____
_____
_____

How God Sees Me

_____
_____
_____
_____
_____
_____
_____
_____

[Jesus answered...]
"I and the Father are one."

John 10:30 **NIV**

She leaned her head against the glass door that led out to the courtyard and watched the rain. She sighed and whispered to herself, "Rain, rain, always rain." She watched the sky weep on the bare earth while the trees, stripped and exposed, drooped with winter's heavy death.

"Lord, why does my spirit feel so stifled with the weight of this season?" her thoughts raced as she whispered to herself. "Everything feels bleak and hopeless. It's as if I'm reaching and reaching, trying to grasp Your robes to keep from falling away. I look for You but then the cares of life scream for my attention. My heart tries to reassure me that You're close, and while I know it's true that You're *always* there, I get sidetracked and distracted. It's as though there's a disconnect between what my heart knows and what my mind comprehends."

As she tried to make sense of her feelings, His perfect Love washed over her and with it, the assurance of His promise that she would soon see tiny leaves appear and flowers burst forth, starting the rebirth of His creation.

She took a deep breath and felt a sunbeam warm her face and chase the darkness from her soul. In her mind's eye, she looked up and beheld the world, cleansed and pure, reborn from the death of winter. Spring would soon be here and with it, Easter! Her soul rejoiced as she whispered to herself, "Hallelujah!"

It all began with a young girl, a Baby, and a Promise.

Then after 400 years of silence, God spoke again
and the Word became flesh.

*The virgin will conceive and give birth to a son, and they
will call him Immanuel (which means "God with Us").*

Matthew 1:23 NIV

He is **The Christ.**   **Messiah.**   **Our Redeemer.**

Your Savior is here. God stepped down from His throne and chose frailty, vulnerability, disappointment, being hated and ostracized, all of which were overshadowed by a deep anguish at seeing His children as lost sheep with no shepherd to care for them. He could have given up, "washed His hands" of His creation, thought you were not worth the effort, but He didn't. He loves you too much. Imagine the depth of love that would cause Someone to embrace the cross.

It's not a fairytale. It's not a story invented by weak people who need a crutch. God the Father, Creator of all things, gave up His throne, took on human form, and came into our world to rescue us. God the Son, Jesus Christ, our Messiah came to show us Who our Heavenly Father is and to open the way of reconciliation.

He came for me. He came for you. He waits with open arms.

Today in the town of David a Savior has been born to you;

He is the Messiah, the Lord.

Luke 2:11 NIV

While they were there,
the time came for the baby to be born,
and she gave birth to her firstborn, a son.
She wrapped him in cloths and placed him in a manger,
because there was no guest room available for them.

Luke 2:6-7 NIV

There she was, just a child, exhausted and shaking, yet exhilarated and entranced, a contradiction of so many feelings she had hidden in her heart since that incredible day the angel had visited her.

And now at last, she let her gaze travel slowly up the precious form of her son, noting the ten perfect toes, the baby softness of tiny arms and legs, the sweet fragrance of his breath marking the rise and fall of his chest in quiet slumber. Up, up, up her eyes went, drinking in every inch of him as she cradled him against her breast. This was ecstasy, the depth of her feelings almost taking her breath away.

As she held him close, she felt the beat of his heart in tandem with hers. He stirred and turned, opening his eyes, and she looked down into…

eternity.

"Why were you searching for me?" he asked,
"Didn't you know I had to be in my Father's house?"

Luke 2:49 NIV

Her eyes darted here and there, frantically searching, searching, "Where did he go, where could he be?" she silently chastised herself. How could she have not known he wasn't with them?

It had been three days, THREE DAYS, since they started back to look for him! Anything could have happened. She prayed silently as she and Joseph questioned others, "Show us, protect him, please help us."

Finally they made it back to the temple, exhausted, spent, their last hope.

Her heart leapt and she clutched Joseph's arm, "There he is, look!" The young boy, sitting with the teachers, was calm, attentive, questioning. With overwhelming relief that overpowered decorum she exclaimed, "Son, why have you treated us like this?"

A quiet answer and further questions drifted away as she considered the implications of her son's explanation. Her confusion softened and then peace welled up within her spirit.

He was her son, carried in her body, fed at her breast, nurtured, and comforted. All the feelings of motherhood tumbled through her heart with lightning speed. He would always be her son, but He was, first of all, His Father's Son, and her unconscious claim on him, her unique position as his mother, while always there, would have to lessen as he became more in tune with his Father's will.

And so, she mentally relinquished her hold and put her faith in God's plan for His Son, her Savior.

*For God so loved the world
that he gave his one and only Son
that whoever believes in him shall not perish
but have eternal life.*

John 3:16 NIV

What do you think it was like in heaven on THAT DAY?

In silence they waited, hovering, intent,
the agony of their stay beyond endurance.

Wings quivering, they strained to loose the Word
that bound them to their places.
Oh, to fly! Wings unrestrained!
White glory sweeping all from their path as they
streamed earthward to rescue
the One who loved beyond measure,
The Bright Morning Star.

But in agony they waited in silence.
The Word that held them was gentle, yet firm.
Even as the earth groaned and writhed in a reflection of His suffering,
it held them to their waiting, and all eternity held its breath…
and waited.

The blackness of sin crashed down upon the bleeding body of one Man
and the earth heaved in its final agony as He released His Spirit.

In awe, the mighty ones looked upon a tomb that was still,
a temporary sleeping place.
Only heaven saw the sights inside that crypt,
as He shed the shackles of humanity
and once again took on the mantle of Divinity.

And as the world slept, not yet aware of His departure,
not comprehending that ultimate freedom was assured,
the mighty ones worshipped the Holy One returned,
as all heaven rejoiced.

Do you ever wonder if, when Adam and Eve ate from the forbidden tree, Jesus immediately turned away and started walking toward the cross?

Jesus is in every book of God's Word. He IS the Word and every word points to the cross. Jesus knew before the foundation of the world what He had to do and He willingly did it for you.

Would you give your life for someone you didn't know? Do you ever wonder at what age Jesus understood His purpose? When He looked into eternity and saw YOU?

You were lost and living a life filled with stuff, all kinds of stuff. You couldn't see anything else…just the stuff of your life: school, work, loved ones, same old, same old. Nothing was necessarily bad, but in the mixture was an empty feeling that there had to be something more. You felt kind of, alone.

Jesus saw that from the cross. He knew that if He made the sacrifice, if He took the punishment meant for you, it would open the way for you to come home to your Heavenly Father forever.

And so it was accomplished, the way back to your Father restored. It's a free gift — a do-over of eternal and infinite proportion.

> *Mercy* means you don't have to take the punishment you deserve. Jesus took the punishment for you.
>
> *Grace* means you are given a priceless gift you do not deserve. That priceless gift is reconciliation and eternal life with God.

> For you. All for you.

You can choose Jesus. The angels in heaven are waiting to greet you. Your Heavenly Father is anxious to welcome you. Will you come?

Pray this prayer with me: *"Lord Jesus, I need You. I'm sorry for all the wrong things I've done and I want to repent and ask You to forgive me. I believe You are God's Son and that You died to save me so I can live with You forever. Please come into my heart, change me, and make me Yours. Amen."*

All heaven celebrates when a wayward child comes home. It's never too late. Jesus told the thief on the cross that he would be in Paradise with Him that very day.

> *"But while he was still a long way off, his father saw him and was filled with compassion for him; he ran to his son, threw his arms around him, and kissed him."*
>
> Luke 15:20 NIV

Like the prodigal's father, You ran to meet me.
Picking up your robes, You disregarded tradition
and only saw my need as You enfolded me
with Your love and acceptance.

The robe with which You covered me to hide the
nakedness of my sin and shame was Grace;
the outside was the brilliant white of purity,
the lining was the scarlet stain of sacrifice.

You came down to the level of my disgrace to welcome me.
You took the mantle of my sin and wore it,
giving me the priceless gift of Your own holiness to wear.

Consequently, you are no longer foreigners and strangers,

but fellow citizens with God's people

and also members of his household,

built on the foundation of the apostles and prophets,

with Christ Jesus himself as the chief cornerstone.

In him the whole building is joined together

and rises to become a holy temple in the Lord.

And in him you too are being built together

to become a dwelling in which God lives by his Spirit.

Ephesians 2:19-22 NIV

When you accepted God's gift of salvation through the sacrifice of His Son, you became part of the family of God.

Your salvation was always part of God's plan! From before the foundation of the world, He chose you to be His child, to be part of His story. He knows you because He designed you perfectly.

> *You clothed me with skin and flesh,*
> *and wove me together*
> *with bones and tendons.*
> *You gave me life and faithful love,*
> *and Your care has guarded my life.*
>
> Job 10:11-12 HCSB

You have His Holy Spirit living in you.

> *Do you not know that your bodies are temples of the Holy Spirit,*
> *who is in you, whom you have received from God?*
> *You are not your own; you were bought at a price.*
> *Therefore honor God with your bodies.*
>
> 1 Corinthians 6:19-20 NIV

You are loved unconditionally by God; you are free to love others, and by doing so, you bring honor to the One who died for you. The love you have for Jesus and others is what sets you apart.

> *This is how we know what love is:*
> *Jesus Christ laid down his life for us.*
> *And we ought to lay down our lives*
> *for our brothers and sisters.*
>
> 1 John 3:16 NIV

I am a Child of God

If you invited Jesus to come into your heart, I rejoice with you! Use this space to record your spiritual birth date and things you would like to remember about this day.

_____

_____

_____

_____

_____

_____

_____

_____

_____

_____

_____

Listen! My beloved!
Look! Here he comes,
leaping across the mountains,
bounding over the hills.

Song of Songs 2:8 *NIV*

As a young man marries
a young woman,
so will your Builder marry you;
as a bridegroom rejoices over his bride,
so will your God rejoice over you.

Isaiah 62:5 *NIV*

She was the prodigal daughter, raised in a Christian home by two amazing parents who loved God, loved each other, and loved their three children. Her childhood was idyllic, not perfect, of course, but pretty close. She knew she was cherished by her parents; maybe she took that for granted. It's just that her life felt so good. Oh, she had the normal angst as she stumbled through those early teenage years into adulthood, but she also had an incredible support system at home. And church. She loved church. She loved the youth group and her friends. She loved church camp and the Easter sunrise service as well, but the Christmas Eve candlelight service was her favorite.

And God? God was Someone she visited every time the church was open, which was fine, but He wasn't Someone she knew intimately, although she had every opportunity. It's just that in those formative years, she didn't make the spiritual connection between what she knew in her head and what was missing in her heart.

So, without totally realizing the dark direction toward which she was heading, she went off to college and promptly went crazy with her newfound "freedom." It's funny, her so-called freedom was her jail sentence. What was her "spunk," her "confidence," her "spiritedness" was really her attempt to skirt the edge of what was right and wrong. But she really didn't think she was a *bad* person. She was a free spirit.

Sadly, she didn't realize she was merrily skipping along a road to nowhere. Her parents were oblivious to the exact danger lurking behind their youngest. They couldn't see the black hand that kept reaching for her; they just routinely did what great parents do, they spent time on their knees.

And so her parents prayed.

As she looks back on her life at that time, she realizes that the prayers of her parents kept her from destroying herself with all the things her "friends" and she were doing.

Her world started shrinking when she, at 20, lost her dad and then flunked out of college. She tried moving to Canada with a boyfriend. Didn't work. Moved back to the U.S. Partied hard. Tripped over her sin and fell in a hole. And now by herself, still her mother prayed.

Suddenly she realized she could fall no further. Her sin, heavy and black, smothered her. She wept, not because she was scared, but because she knew in her heart that she had no one she could call to make her feel better. No person, no drug, no drink; she was "naked" with nothing to hide behind and cowering in a hole she had dug herself. The TV was on some vague station — an evangelist, of all things. She half-listened and then she heard her name. Someone was promising her eternal love and mercy. It was Jesus! Jesus was calling her! He reached in, took hold of her heart, marrying it with the spiritual head knowledge and example her parents had given her as a child, then lifted her out of that hole of self-destruction, and saved her.

Her parents had prayed; her mother continued praying; Jesus found her.

> *For by grace you have been saved through faith,*
> *and that is not of yourselves; it is the gift of God,*
> *not by works, lest anyone should boast.*

> Ephesians 2:8 NKJV

Surely your goodness and love will follow me all the days of my life, and I will dwell in the house of the LORD forever.

Psalm 23:6 NIV

> *"Then the angel showed me the river of the water of life,*
> *as clear as crystal, flowing from the throne of God*
> *and of the Lamb down the middle of the great street of the city.*
> *On each side of the river stood the tree of life,*
> *bearing twelve crops of fruit, yielding its fruit every month.*
> *And the leaves of the tree are for the healing of the nations.*
> *No longer will there be any curse. The throne of God and*
> *of the Lamb will be in the city, and his servants will serve him.*
> *They will see his face, and his name will be on their foreheads.*
> *There will be no more night. They will not need the light*
> *of a lamp or the light of the sun, for the Lord God*
> *will give them light. And they will reign for ever and ever."*
>
> Revelation 22:1-5 NIV

The Promise. Your Savior will not forsake you. He is preparing a special place for the children of God. You can live without fear of the unknown. Your Shepherd knows you and you know His voice. When the final trumpet sounds, the Lord will gather all the redeemed to life everlasting.

Your life here, as a beloved child of the King, is only a dim reflection of the glory that will surround you as you drink in the beauty of Paradise and behold your Lord and Savior Immanuel.

He is Perfect Love. Whisper some of His Names as you worship:

KING of KINGS   **LORD of LORDS**

              GOOD SHEPHERD

SAVIOR   **IMMANUEL**

              WORD of GOD

ALPHA and OMEGA   **ALMIGHTY GOD**

*For now we see only a reflection as in a mirror;
then we shall see face to face. Now I know in part;
then I shall know fully even as I am fully known.*

1 Corinthians 13:12 NIV

Ishi

a Biblical name that means
SALVATION

A beloved's name, a term of endearment.
The One to whom you gave your heart.
Jesus, your Salvation.
He is the Bridegroom who will come back for His bride.

All creation and the redeemed are anxiously awaiting the day.

*We know that the whole creation has been groaning
as in the pains of childbirth right up to the present time.
Not only so, but we ourselves, who have the first fruits
of the Spirit, groan inwardly as we wait eagerly
for our adoption to sonship, the redemption of our bodies.*

Romans 8:22-23 NIV

And we shall see Him as He is.

*Dear friends, now we are children of God,
and what we will be has not yet been made known.
But we know that when Christ appears,
we shall be like him, for we shall see him as he is.*

1 John 3:2 NIV

My hopes and dreams for my life

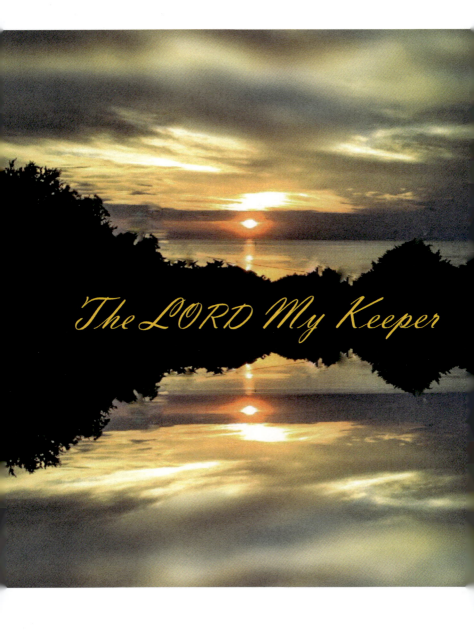

I lift up my eyes to the mountains—
where does my help come from?
My help comes from the LORD,
the Maker of heaven and earth.
He will not let your foot slip—
he who watches over you
will not slumber; indeed,
he who watches over Israel
will neither slumber nor sleep.
The LORD watches over you—
the LORD is your shade
at your right hand;
the sun will not harm you by day,
nor the moon by night
The LORD will keep you from all harm—
he will watch over your life;
the LORD will watch over your coming
and going both now and forevermore.

Psalm 121:1-8 **NIV**

Lover of my Soul, Keeper of my Heart

Your Father delights in you. He is your Keeper and your Protector.

In the book of Hosea, the Israelites continually turned their backs on the One True God and adopted the idols of the pagan cultures around them. Think about that and compare it to our culture today. What are our idols? Are there things that keep our attention so preoccupied we neglect our relationship with our Heavenly Father? Even "good deeds" can sometimes monopolize our lives to the extent that we put them before God.

Your Father is your first Love. He has given you His Holy Spirit to lead you to areas of service in His Name. With His leading, the things you do will have eternal value. Every joy you experience, every challenge, every trial can result in beauty because you have been obedient, beauty because your goal has been to honor your Lord and Savior, and beauty because you've made a positive difference in someone's life by loving and serving them in Jesus's Name.

> *He brought me out into a spacious place;*
> *he rescued me because he delighted in me.*
>
> Psalm 18:19 NIV

Wild flowers growing along fences; Perfect roses in wedding bouquets; Easter lilies lining church altars in the spring. Each one beautiful in its own way.

You are like a precious flower, unique and cherished by the One who created you and loves you. Embrace your uniqueness as a gift from Him. He has chosen you to be an integral part of His story.

He knew you before you were yet a thought. He planned your place in history, planned where you would live, who your family would be, what you would look like. No detail was missed. He gave you a mind, a heart, a soul, and, because He wanted you to love Him without coercion, He gave you the freedom to reject not just all the beautiful things He lavished on you, but also Him.

It's your choice; it always has been. He made every provision possible so you could come back to Him.

All through history, He has sent messages of His love through the things He created. Remember that beautiful sunset you saw the other evening? That was a love letter from Him. The birds outside your window this morning? They were singing His love song to you.

He has done everything possible to woo you, to assure you of His love, to win your heart. He even gave up heaven to come and rescue you. He took the blame for all your mistakes and then he embraced the punishment meant for you. He loves you that much. It's never too late to accept His mercy and grace. Just whisper, "Jesus."

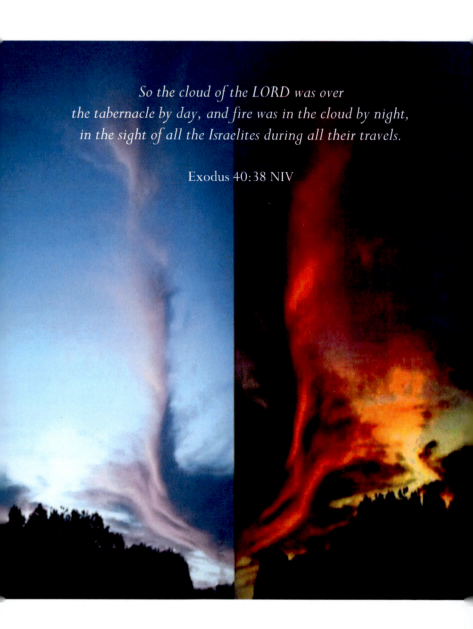

*So the cloud of the LORD was over
the tabernacle by day, and fire was in the cloud by night,
in the sight of all the Israelites during all their travels.*

Exodus 40:38 NIV

Desert Wanderings

Because of your great compassion you did not abandon them in the wilderness. By day the pillar of cloud did not fail to guide them on their path, nor the pillar of fire by night to shine on the way they were to take.

Nehemiah 9:19 NIV

She walked, then ran, then stopped and bent over to catch her breath. Hands on knees, she heaved and gulped in great mouthfuls of air. Tears streamed down her face as she frantically searched for what was just beyond her reach. "I need to rest," she decided. "This is going nowhere. Maybe if I watch a Christmas movie or work on Christmas cards." Her mind jumped ahead, "I still need to make jam and fudge, oh, and cookies! I really want to make Christmas cookies." Reluctantly, but in a way relieved, she stopped obsessing and immersed herself in activities; admirable activities, she thought, things she would do for others…good activities, noble and unselfish activities.

Unfortunately, all too soon she found herself running again, searching again. "Why am I so tired, "she muttered to herself. "Why can't I find it *and* WHAT IS IT?" That thing, that something she couldn't name, but for which she had been searching, that thing she had lost or misplaced, was fuzzy in her mind and just beyond her reach. Oh, she had been busy watching all the beautiful Christmas movies, reading her favorite author's latest book, shopping online for Christmas presents. She had enjoyed Christmas programs, sung on Sunday with the choir, attended Christmas parties, all the while yearning for that THING she had lost and wishing she knew what it was! "Maybe," she thought, "I can retrace my steps, go back to the last time I was happy. I might have dropped it somewhere along the way, whatever IT is. Oh, I hate feeling this way!" she mentally stomped her foot.

"I remember my affliction
and my wandering,
the bitterness and the gall.
 I well remember them,
and my soul is downcast within me.
Yet this I call to mind
and therefore I have hope…"

Lamentations 3:19-21 NIV

That was it. She was at the end of her rope. Christmas was coming and she didn't care. She really just wanted to crawl in a hole. All her activities, cooking, cleaning, decorating, choir practice, didn't contain the thing she needed most, that *something* she had lost or misplaced or dropped. She gave up.

"It's gone," she whispered to herself. "I'll never find it, whatever IT is; I'll never get it back."

"Look inside."

"What?"

"Stop and look inside."

"Look inside for what? What is it?"

"It's what you've been looking for — what you thought you'd lost. It's Me."

(She was feeling really dumb now. How could she have been so blind? The answer had been in her the whole time. She had pushed it away and replaced it with THINGS that made her feel good.)

"I'm sorry, I'm so sorry. I'm miserable and now I know why. Forgive me. Help me. Don't leave me."

"I will never leave you, nor will I forsake you. You don't have to look outside for me. Look inside. Stop running. Breathe in and let My Spirit fill you. Only then will you find satisfaction and meaning for your life. Only then can the excess of My love overflow onto others with whom you come in contact. You're My precious child. I designed you to be a light to others but unless you make room for Me first, that light will fail and you'll find yourself in darkness, lost and unable to find your way. I'm in you. Leave the past in the past and stop worrying about the things you feel you need to do. You will always find Me in the present. I wait here for you."

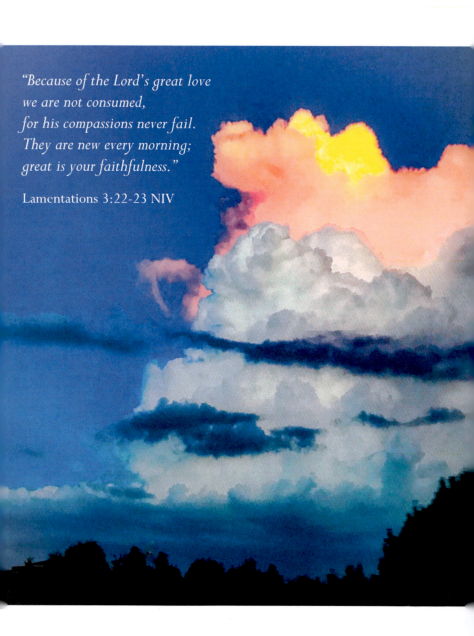

"Because of the Lord's great love
we are not consumed,
for his compassions never fail.
They are new every morning;
great is your faithfulness."

Lamentations 3:22-23 NIV

"How could I have been so out of touch? I must have been so caught up in DOING that I forgot about BEING," her heart melted with relief as love for her Lord flooded through her, and she shook her head, always amazed and humbled at His love for her. "Thank You, Lord, for not giving up on me. Thank You for forgiving me, saving me, and showing me how to find You when I've wandered off Your path."

> *Can a mother forget the baby at her breast and have no compassion on the child she has borne? Though she may forget, I will not forget you! See, I have engraved you on the palms of my hands; your walls are ever before me.*
>
> Isaiah 49:15-16 NIV

> *You will seek me and find me when you seek me with all your heart.*
>
> Jeremiah 29:13 NIV

> *For I am convinced that neither death nor life, neither angels nor demons, neither the present nor the future, nor any powers, neither height nor depth, nor anything else in all creation, will be able to separate us from the love of God that is in Christ Jesus our Lord.*
>
> Romans 8:38-39 NIV

Every rainbow is a promise of God, established at the beginning of creation. Then, it was a covenant between Him and His creation. Today, it represents the same covenant and reminds us of His faithfulness, His love, and His promises. HE NEVER CHANGES.

> *Heaven and earth will pass away,*
> *but my words will never pass away.*
>
> Luke 21:33 NIV

The Lord promises to never leave nor forsake us. He promises that His plans for us are good. He promises that He will never allow us to be tempted beyond what we can overcome with His help. Sometimes we don't see His hand on our lives until we've traveled way past the circumstance but just like He did with Peter, He will walk beside us in our storms and support us.

Read His Word. Write down and memorize His promises. At times, reciting a promise of God to yourself is all you need to give you the courage to go on. God's Word is alive and will minister to you in different ways at different times. It's always fresh, always applicable to your current situation, and always, ALWAYS the Truth.

> *For the word of God is alive and active.*
> *Sharper than any double-edged sword, it penetrates*
> *even to dividing soul and spirit, joints and marrow;*
> *it judges the thoughts and attitudes of the heart.*
>
> Hebrews 4:12 NIV

God's Promises to Me

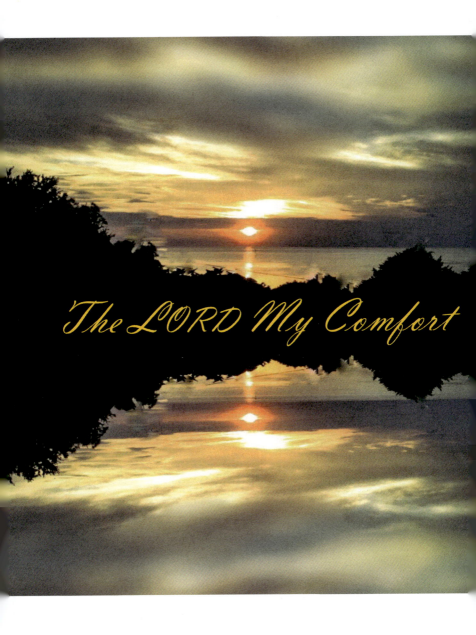

Even though I walk through

the darkest valley,

I will fear no evil,

for you are with me;

your rod and your staff,

they comfort me.

Psalm 23:4 **NIV**

The valley of the shadow of death can be such a frightening, overwhelming place!

Take a moment to savor David's 23rd psalm. It's a sweet reflection of our Father's care of us. We are so much like sheep — helpless, easily distracted, timid. David uses the different ways he takes care of his own flock to describe how God takes care of him (and us).

Sometimes we have to be in the middle of a crisis to remember God, to cry out to Him for help. Maybe we try to convince ourselves He really wants to help us. I mean, is our problem really serious enough for Him?

David starts his Psalm describing God in the third person. *"He* makes me lie down…*He* leads me…*He* restores." Then from the fourth verse to the end, he switches to more intimate wording. "Even though I walk through the darkest valley, I will fear no evil, for *you* are with me; *your* rod and *your* staff, they comfort me. *You* prepare a table before me in the presence of my enemies. *You* anoint my head with oil; my cup overflows…" The more we focus on God as we pick our way through the sometimes minefield of our lives, the closer we get to Him and the more we see that we **can** trust Him with every aspect of our lives. Nothing is too small or outside the realm of His concern.

Jesus is the Good Shepherd and we are His sheep. Because we belong to Him, we recognize His voice when He speaks to us through His Holy Spirit. *He* is our Protector, our Comfort, the One Who guides us through our darkest valleys. When we were lost, He searched and found us, giving the ultimate sacrifice of His life to ensure our freedom from death. And now, when we find ourselves standing at the threshold of *our* dark valley, our Shepherd's love and guidance bring comfort and hope.

I am the good shepherd; I know my sheep and my sheep know me—
just as the Father knows me and I know the Father—
and I lay down my life for the sheep."

John 10:14-15 NIV

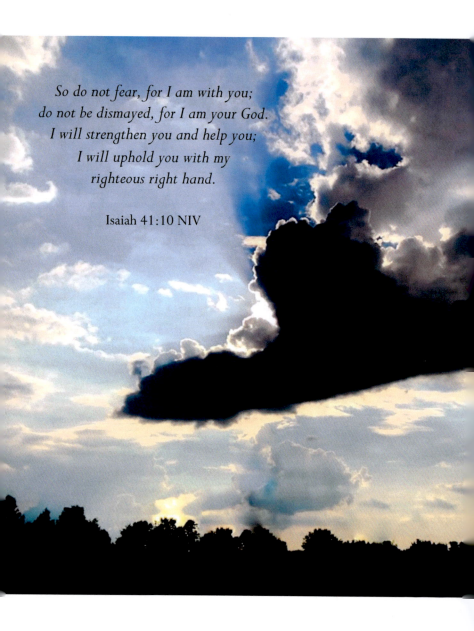

"You Have Cancer"

That word drew a line, a line that divided her life between:

        "BC"   Before cancer

and

        "LC"   Living with cancer

The fear, hidden deep down inside her spirit, suddenly burst to the surface. Her mind went into overdrive as she tried to come to grips with what this news meant for her life. Memories washed over her: first, her sweet dad. She unconsciously shuddered as she recalled the cancer that took his life so long ago. And her sister, whose cancer was discovered in time and God healed her. "Now," she thought, "now it's my turn."

The next days were a blur. Doctors, decisions, dates…all necessary, all confusing, all scary. Should she quit her job? "One day at a time, honey," her husband reassured her. "We'll get through this."

And so she tried to focus on the here and now. Recuperating from major surgery took a lot of energy. She took baby steps and wondered what her life was going to look like.

There were days she went through on autopilot: work, chemotherapy, doctor's appointments. So many unfamiliar things, things that were now part of her life. She was tired all the time; her hair was gone; food tasted terrible, her body ached. At times, she felt like she was on the outside looking in, watching someone else's journey. She wanted to wake up from this dream but she couldn't. Her focus became inward, her life revolved around **her** health, **her** comfort, **her** prognosis. Where would it end? She was no longer sure of her place, where she fit in.

Because I, your GOD, have a firm grip on you and I'm not letting go. I'm telling you, "Don't panic. I'm right here to help you."

Isaiah 41:13 MSG

And then the day came. "I CAN'T DO THIS!" (wailing silently to herself). And finally, the question to God, "WHY ME, LORD?"

The voice impressed on her heart was soft and loving, "Why not you?"

That made her stop. She took a deep breath, let it out, and then remembered the Bible study she had started the night before her surgery. So long ago it seemed. What was it about? It wasn't about me? Ohhh, yes. She had been so consumed with her health, she'd forgotten how to live for God. In all her running, running, running, she'd left God behind.

WOW.

She took another breath and focused on her Heavenly Father, her Savior. She sought Him out, searched for His heart, and little by little, she relinquished her death grip on her life and let Him take over. It wasn't easy; many times it was frightening. But deep inside, she knew if she'd let Him, He would lead her to a new level of relationship with Him. Intimate.

The peace didn't come right away but it was such a relief to know she had Someone else fighting her battles. And her focus slowly started turning outward. She became aware of others fighting similar battles and her life intersected with people who needed a touch of hope, something God was giving her to share.

It was a turning point, that exact moment when GOD STEPPED IN. He taught her how to minister to others. He also showed her the importance of allowing others to minister to her. And slowly but steadily she learned what it meant to be the hands and feet of Jesus.

Was there suffering she had yet to experience? Yes, but somehow, knowing that Someone else had also suffered made the thought of possible unpleasant things to come more bearable. Fear of the unknown could be overwhelming, the "what if" questions debilitating.

There was a particular time when she was in despair and cried out to God for help. He answered her in Psalm 18 and as she read it for the first time, she felt an incredible peace and delight. She pictured God, her Father; God, her Rescuer; God, her Hero — the ultimate Hero — coming to save her. He was the One who loved her beyond measure, the One who delighted in her, the One who cherished her. It was only when she was in Him that she felt completely safe from all fear and worry.

"In my distress I called to the Lord; I cried to my God for help. From his temple he heard my voice; my cry came before him, into his ears. The earth trembled and quaked, and the foundations of the mountains shook; they trembled because he was angry. Smoke rose from his nostrils; consuming fire came from his mouth, burning coals blazed out of it. He parted the heavens and came down; dark clouds were under his feet. He mounted the cherubim and flew; he soared on the wings of the wind. He made darkness his covering, his canopy around him— the dark rain clouds of the sky. Out of the brightness of his presence clouds advanced, with hailstones and bolts of lightning. The Lord thundered from heaven; the voice of the Most High resounded. He shot his arrows and scattered the enemy, with great bolts of lightning he routed them. The valleys of the sea were exposed and the foundations of the earth laid bare at your rebuke, Lord, at the blast of breath from your nostrils. He reached down from on high and took hold of me; he drew me out of deep waters. He rescued me from my powerful enemy, from my foes, who were too strong for me. They confronted me in the day of my disaster, but the Lord was my support. He brought me out into a spacious place; he rescued me because he delighted in me." Psalm 18:6-19 NIV

"Coping and Continuing"

SURVIVOR'S GUILT

As she continued on her journey of "new normalcy," at times she found herself experiencing what she called "survivor's guilt." It was hard to lose friends to cancer. She found herself wondering why God took them and not her. And then she would wonder if the family of the one who passed resented her for still being alive. It was a strange burden to carry.

Irrational? Probably. Silly? Perhaps. Real? Yes.

She was talking to a dear friend about a sweet saint who had recently been called home and she was explaining the "survivor's guilt" phenomenon. She wasn't feeling sorry for herself. It was just something she was trying to understand in the context of her own illness.

Suddenly, she felt a very distinct impression of her Heavenly Father whispering to her heart.

"Honey, please don't question My plan for your life."

With relief, she gave up that burden and continued on, walking every day, husband by her side, hand-in-hand with her Heavenly Father, feeling great joy in the midst of a sometimes painful reality. A day-by-day journey of choosing to let go of concerns and fears and depend on God to lead her faithfully, graciously, and lovingly over the rough terrain of the unknown.

But I am like an olive tree flourishing in the house of God;
I trust in God's unfailing love for ever and ever.

Psalm 52:8 NIV

And now, 15 years later...

Today, as the Lord comforts her, He shows her how to use her experiences to comfort others who are going through their own valleys. When she does, when she reaches out to others with love and concern, that gesture gives her trial eternal significance, bringing something positive out of something that is negative.

Now she can see there are many opportunities to respond positively to the challenge of living with cancer and being a cancer survivor. She understands that her responses have eternal implications. She can choose to hide behind her fear and become inwardly focused or she can give her life away to the One who has given her everything.

How can she ignore so great a sacrifice that was given without requiring anything in return? She had accepted the gift of His mercy and grace lavished on her so long ago. Can she now comprehend what He did for her and allow Him to use her life however He wishes?

It's a daily choice to put His plan before her desires. It's confusing, frustrating, and she fails miserably at times. But it's worth it.

"How priceless is your unfailing love, O God!
People take refuge in the shadow of your wings."

Psalm 36:7 NIV

"Take my life, use me up, show me the blackness of my soul without the illuminating presence of Your forgiving Spirit so that I will see and understand Your amazing grace. I don't want to spend one second outside of Your will and plan for my life."

Amen.

Comfort I get from God's Word

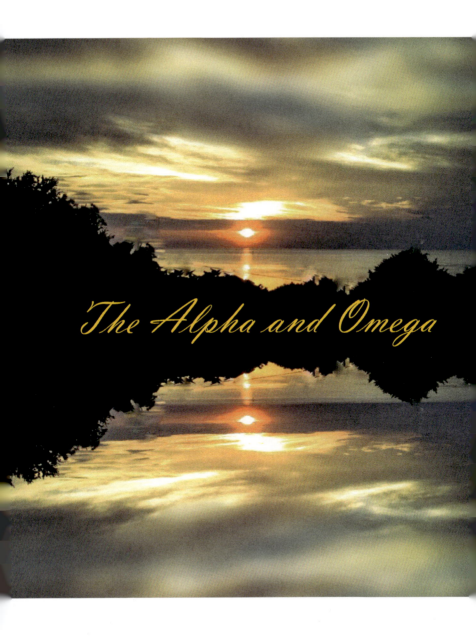

...and from Jesus Christ,

who is the faithful witness

the firstborn from the dead,

and the ruler of the kings of the earth.

To him who loves us and has

freed us from our sins by his blood,

and has made us to be a kingdom and priests

to serve his God and Father—

to him be glory and power

forever and ever! Amen.

Revelation 1:5-6 *NIV*

Her Wedding

When she was young, it was a dream of Cinderella proportions. Beautiful bride in a bejeweled white gown with a train, a tiara with a veil that cascaded over her shoulders and down her back, white roses, handsome groom, being loved, living happily ever after.

It would truly be a fairytale life.

She found her handsome prince. With God's help.

Right after she gave her heart to Jesus, she went to the altar and prayed that God would start preparing her heart and the heart of the man He had chosen for her. Three years later, she fell in love at first sight and married her best friend.

And they lived happily ever after, as God taught them what it meant to "forsake all others" and be who He had created them to be in marriage. They learned what it meant to put God first and sacrifice their own desires for the good of the other. They learned that it wasn't about each separate person. The two had become one and God was the Head. That was the most important lesson they learned, sometimes the hard way, after many trials. But they came to understand that anything valuable to God was worth any price they had to pay.

So it was a daily giving up of pride, the strong-willed desire to get one's way or always be right. It was no longer "his or her way." It was always God's way.

That was 40 years ago, and she is more in love with her prince than she was the day they married.

One man and one woman,
starting out as two hearts,
are fashioned so carefully by God
that one cannot be whole without the other!

At birth, both hearts are linked to each other
with the scarlet thread from One Life,
but they are still two incomplete parts.
One heart is a lock without a key,
the other a key alone.

In separate existence,
one heart beats a dim echo of the other,
while the fluctuations of living cause the
Life-thread joining the two to tangle and knot,

Now the way to each other is so hidden
that only by following the scarlet thread
back to the One Life can the pattern emerge:
two hearts, finally side by side,
joined by and reflecting the image of One Heart,
the only Doorway to each other.

The two hearts are now so completely joined
that one sustains the other,
strength lifting weakness, laughter drying tears;
souls never parted but held fast,
two hearts forever beating in One!

*I saw the Holy City, the new Jerusalem
coming down out of heaven from God,
prepared as a bride beautifully dressed for her husband.*

Revelation 21:2 NIV

"Do not let your hearts be troubled. You believe in God;
believe also in me. My Father's house has many rooms;
if that were not so, would I have told you
that I am going there to prepare a place for you?
And if I go and prepare a place for you,
I will come back and take you to be with me
that you also may be where I am."

John 14:1-3 NIV

The Wedding

As she looks back on her marriage, she knows that she was and is being prepared to be the Bride of the Lamb of God. Jesus, her Savior has gone ahead to make sure everything will be perfect for His Bride, the body of believers, the children of God, her. It will be a glorious celebration.

Blessed are those who wash their robes,
that they may have the right to the tree of life
and may go through the gates into the city.
The Spirit and the bride say, "Come!"
And let the one who hears say, "Come!"
Let the one who is thirsty come;
and let the one who wishes
take the free gift of the water of life.

Revelation 22:14,17 NIV

It's not too late. Won't you come? He's waiting with open arms.

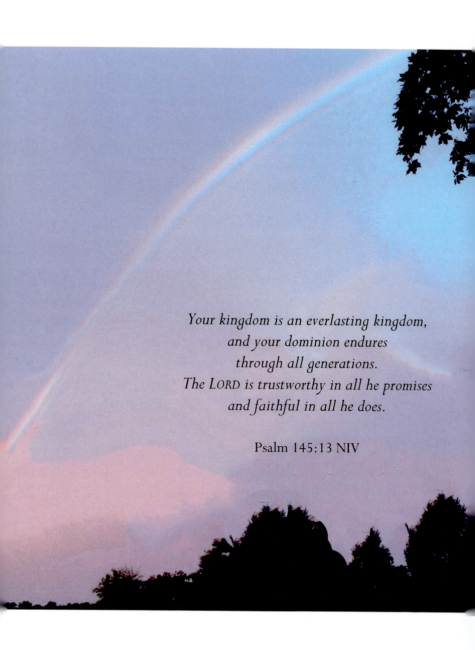

> *"I am the Alpha and the Omega, the First and the Last, the Beginning and the End."*
>
> Revelation 22:13 HCSB

Dear Heavenly Father,

You promise in Your Word to honor obedience. Help me always walk in the footsteps of Your Son Jesus. Give me the courage to take steps of faith and the wisdom to discern the path You've set before me.

Thank you that even when my circumstances may cause me fear, I have the assurance that my victory is in Christ. I only have to do what is right — what Jesus would do — and place my trust in You.

Let my life count for You. Help me love others the way You love them. Protect me from hurt feelings and show me how to help others be the best they can be.

And finally, Father, help me take time to listen to Your Holy Spirit. Empty me of thoughts that keep me from receiving all that would make me totally Yours. Illuminate my understanding and open my mind and heart to appreciate the beauty of Your creation so I can glorify You and give You the honor You alone deserve.

I pray this in the matchless Name of Jesus.

Amen.

Made in the USA
San Bernardino,
CA